THIS SWIMMING JOURNAL BELONGS TO

"Swimmers don't quit.
Quitters don't swim."

TABLE OF CONTENTS

Training Log 1

Personal Records 101

Notes 117

TRAINING LOG

Date: 1/29/28   Time: 7:30

Warm Up

Swim Activity	Distance	Reps	Time	Rest
Free/back	300			

Sets

Swim Activity	Distance	Reps	Time	Rest
4(Kick/D/swim	75	4	(300)	:10
FAST KICK	25	8	(200)	
100 IM	100	1		
100 SWIM	100	1		
100 IM	100	1		
200 FREE	200	1		
100 IM	100	1		
300 FREE	300	1		
100 IM	100	1		
400 FREE	400	1		
100 IM	100	1		
500 Free	500	1		

Pull
Pull
Pull
Pull

Cool Down

Swim Activity	Distance	Reps	Time	Rest
50	50	1		

2850

Difficulty: Rating: ★ ★ ★ ★

1

TRAINING LOG

Date: 1/31   Time: 7:00

Warm Up

Swim Activity	Distance	Reps	Time	Rest
3 00				

Sets

Swim Activity	Distance	Reps	Time	Rest
Kick	50	8		
Swim free	100	8		
Swim Free	200	4		
Swim Free	400	2		
3400 m				

Cool Down

Swim Activity	Distance	Reps	Time	Rest
	100			

Difficulty: 🏊 🏊 🏊   Rating: ⭐ ⭐ ⭐ ⭐ ⭐

2

TRAINING LOG

Date: _____ Time: _____

Warm Up

Swim Activity	Distance	Reps	Time	Rest

Sets

Swim Activity	Distance	Reps	Time	Rest

Cool Down

Swim Activity	Distance	Reps	Time	Rest

Difficulty: 🏊 🏊 🏊   Rating: ⭐ ⭐ ⭐ ⭐ ⭐

TRAINING LOG

Date: _____ Time: _____

Warm Up

Swim Activity	Distance	Reps	Time	Rest

Sets

Swim Activity	Distance	Reps	Time	Rest

Cool Down

Swim Activity	Distance	Reps	Time	Rest

Difficulty: 🏊 🏊 🏊   Rating: ⭐ ⭐ ⭐ ⭐ ⭐

── TRAINING LOG ──

Date: _____ Time: _____

Warm Up

Swim Activity	Distance	Reps	Time	Rest

Sets

Swim Activity	Distance	Reps	Time	Rest

Cool Down

Swim Activity	Distance	Reps	Time	Rest

Difficulty: 🏊 🏊 🏊   Rating: ★ ★ ★ ★ ★

TRAINING LOG

Date: _____ Time: _____

Warm Up

Swim Activity	Distance	Reps	Time	Rest

Sets

Swim Activity	Distance	Reps	Time	Rest

Cool Down

Swim Activity	Distance	Reps	Time	Rest

Difficulty: 🏊 🏊 🏊   Rating: ⭐ ⭐ ⭐ ⭐ ⭐

TRAINING LOG

Date: _____ Time: _____

Warm Up

Swim Activity	Distance	Reps	Time	Rest

Sets

Swim Activity	Distance	Reps	Time	Rest

Cool Down

Swim Activity	Distance	Reps	Time	Rest

Difficulty: 🏊 🏊 🏊   Rating: ⭐ ⭐ ⭐ ⭐ ⭐

TRAINING LOG

Date: _____ Time: _____

Warm Up

Swim Activity	Distance	Reps	Time	Rest

Sets

Swim Activity	Distance	Reps	Time	Rest

Cool Down

Swim Activity	Distance	Reps	Time	Rest

Difficulty: 🏊 🏊 🏊   Rating: ⭐ ⭐ ⭐ ⭐ ⭐

TRAINING LOG

Date: _____ Time: _____

Warm Up

Swim Activity	Distance	Reps	Time	Rest

Sets

Swim Activity	Distance	Reps	Time	Rest

Cool Down

Swim Activity	Distance	Reps	Time	Rest

Difficulty: 🏊 🏊 🏊   Rating: ⭐ ⭐ ⭐ ⭐ ⭐

TRAINING LOG

Date: _____ Time: _____

Warm Up

Swim Activity	Distance	Reps	Time	Rest

Sets

Swim Activity	Distance	Reps	Time	Rest

Cool Down

Swim Activity	Distance	Reps	Time	Rest

Difficulty: 🏊 🏊 🏊   Rating: ⭐ ⭐ ⭐ ⭐ ⭐

TRAINING LOG

Date: _____ Time: _____

Warm Up

Swim Activity	Distance	Reps	Time	Rest

Sets

Swim Activity	Distance	Reps	Time	Rest

Cool Down

Swim Activity	Distance	Reps	Time	Rest

Difficulty: 🏊 🏊 🏊 🏊   Rating: ⭐ ⭐ ⭐ ⭐ ⭐

TRAINING LOG

Date: _____ Time: _____

Warm Up

Swim Activity	Distance	Reps	Time	Rest

Sets

Swim Activity	Distance	Reps	Time	Rest

Cool Down

Swim Activity	Distance	Reps	Time	Rest

Difficulty: 🏊 🏊 🏊 Rating: ★ ★ ★ ★ ★

TRAINING LOG ——

Date: _____ Time: _____

Warm Up

Swim Activity	Distance	Reps	Time	Rest

Sets

Swim Activity	Distance	Reps	Time	Rest

Cool Down

Swim Activity	Distance	Reps	Time	Rest

Difficulty: 🏊 🏊 🏊 Rating: ⭐ ⭐ ⭐ ⭐ ⭐

TRAINING LOG

Date: _____ Time: _____

Warm Up

Swim Activity	Distance	Reps	Time	Rest

Sets

Swim Activity	Distance	Reps	Time	Rest

Cool Down

Swim Activity	Distance	Reps	Time	Rest

Difficulty: 🏊 🏊 🏊   Rating: ⭐ ⭐ ⭐ ⭐ ⭐

TRAINING LOG

Date: _____ Time: _____

Warm Up

Swim Activity	Distance	Reps	Time	Rest

Sets

Swim Activity	Distance	Reps	Time	Rest

Cool Down

Swim Activity	Distance	Reps	Time	Rest

Difficulty: 🏊 🏊 🏊   15   Rating: ⭐ ⭐ ⭐ ⭐ ⭐

TRAINING LOG

Date: _____ Time: _____

Warm Up

Swim Activity	Distance	Reps	Time	Rest

Sets

Swim Activity	Distance	Reps	Time	Rest

Cool Down

Swim Activity	Distance	Reps	Time	Rest

Difficulty: ☆ ☆ ☆   Rating: ☆ ☆ ☆ ☆ ☆

TRAINING LOG ——

Date: _____ Time: _____

Warm Up

Swim Activity	Distance	Reps	Time	Rest

Sets

Swim Activity	Distance	Reps	Time	Rest

Cool Down

Swim Activity	Distance	Reps	Time	Rest

Difficulty: 🏊 🏊 🏊   17   Rating: ⭐ ⭐ ⭐ ⭐ ⭐

TRAINING LOG

Date: _____ Time: _____

Warm Up

Swim Activity	Distance	Reps	Time	Rest

Sets

Swim Activity	Distance	Reps	Time	Rest

Cool Down

Swim Activity	Distance	Reps	Time	Rest

Difficulty: 🏊 🏊 🏊   Rating: ⭐ ⭐ ⭐ ⭐ ⭐

TRAINING LOG

Date: _____ Time: _____

Warm Up

Swim Activity	Distance	Reps	Time	Rest

Sets

Swim Activity	Distance	Reps	Time	Rest

Cool Down

Swim Activity	Distance	Reps	Time	Rest

Difficulty: 🏊 🏊 🏊 19 Rating: ⭐ ⭐ ⭐ ⭐ ⭐

TRAINING LOG

Date: _____ Time: _____

Warm Up

Swim Activity	Distance	Reps	Time	Rest

Sets

Swim Activity	Distance	Reps	Time	Rest

Cool Down

Swim Activity	Distance	Reps	Time	Rest

Difficulty: 🏊 🏊 🏊   Rating: ⭐ ⭐ ⭐ ⭐ ⭐

TRAINING LOG

Date: _____ Time: _____

Warm Up

Swim Activity	Distance	Reps	Time	Rest

Sets

Swim Activity	Distance	Reps	Time	Rest

Cool Down

Swim Activity	Distance	Reps	Time	Rest

Difficulty: 🏊 🏊 🏊   Rating: ⭐ ⭐ ⭐ ⭐ ⭐

TRAINING LOG

Date: _____ Time: _____

Warm Up

Swim Activity	Distance	Reps	Time	Rest

Sets

Swim Activity	Distance	Reps	Time	Rest

Cool Down

Swim Activity	Distance	Reps	Time	Rest

Difficulty: 🏊 🏊 🏊   22   Rating: ⭐ ⭐ ⭐ ⭐ ⭐

TRAINING LOG

Date: _____ Time: _____

Warm Up

Swim Activity	Distance	Reps	Time	Rest

Sets

Swim Activity	Distance	Reps	Time	Rest

Cool Down

Swim Activity	Distance	Reps	Time	Rest

Difficulty: 🏊 🏊 🏊 23 Rating: ⭐ ⭐ ⭐ ⭐ ⭐

TRAINING LOG

Date: _____ Time: _____

Warm Up

Swim Activity	Distance	Reps	Time	Rest

Sets

Swim Activity	Distance	Reps	Time	Rest

Cool Down

Swim Activity	Distance	Reps	Time	Rest

Difficulty: 🏊 🏊 🏊   Rating: ⭐ ⭐ ⭐ ⭐ ⭐

TRAINING LOG ——

Date: _____ Time: _____

Warm Up

Swim Activity	Distance	Reps	Time	Rest

Sets

Swim Activity	Distance	Reps	Time	Rest

Cool Down

Swim Activity	Distance	Reps	Time	Rest

Difficulty: 🏊 🏊 🏊 Rating: ⭐ ⭐ ⭐ ⭐ ⭐

TRAINING LOG

Date: _____ Time: _____

Warm Up

Swim Activity	Distance	Reps	Time	Rest

Sets

Swim Activity	Distance	Reps	Time	Rest

Cool Down

Swim Activity	Distance	Reps	Time	Rest

Difficulty: 🏊 🏊 🏊   Rating: ⭐ ⭐ ⭐ ⭐ ⭐

TRAINING LOG

Date: _____ Time: _____

Warm Up

Swim Activity	Distance	Reps	Time	Rest

Sets

Swim Activity	Distance	Reps	Time	Rest

Cool Down

Swim Activity	Distance	Reps	Time	Rest

Difficulty: 🏊 🏊 🏊   Rating: ⭐ ⭐ ⭐ ⭐ ⭐

TRAINING LOG

Date: _____ Time: _____

Warm Up

Swim Activity	Distance	Reps	Time	Rest

Sets

Swim Activity	Distance	Reps	Time	Rest

Cool Down

Swim Activity	Distance	Reps	Time	Rest

Difficulty: 🏊 🏊 🏊

Rating: ⭐ ⭐ ⭐ ⭐ ⭐

— TRAINING LOG —

Date: _____ Time: _____

Warm Up

Swim Activity	Distance	Reps	Time	Rest

Sets

Swim Activity	Distance	Reps	Time	Rest

Cool Down

Swim Activity	Distance	Reps	Time	Rest

Difficulty: 🏊 🏊 🏊   Rating: ⭐ ⭐ ⭐ ⭐ ⭐

TRAINING LOG

Date: _____ Time: _____

Warm Up

Swim Activity	Distance	Reps	Time	Rest

Sets

Swim Activity	Distance	Reps	Time	Rest

Cool Down

Swim Activity	Distance	Reps	Time	Rest

Difficulty: 🏊 🏊 🏊 Rating: ⭐ ⭐ ⭐ ⭐ ⭐

TRAINING LOG

Date: _____ Time: _____

Warm Up				
Swim Activity	Distance	Reps	Time	Rest

Sets				
Swim Activity	Distance	Reps	Time	Rest

Cool Down				
Swim Activity	Distance	Reps	Time	Rest

Difficulty: 🏊 🏊 🏊   Rating: ⭐ ⭐ ⭐ ⭐ ⭐

TRAINING LOG

Date: _____ Time: _____

Warm Up

Swim Activity	Distance	Reps	Time	Rest

Sets

Swim Activity	Distance	Reps	Time	Rest

Cool Down

Swim Activity	Distance	Reps	Time	Rest

Difficulty: 🏊 🏊 🏊   Rating: ⭐ ⭐ ⭐ ⭐ ⭐

TRAINING LOG

Date: _____ Time: _____

Warm Up

Swim Activity	Distance	Reps	Time	Rest

Sets

Swim Activity	Distance	Reps	Time	Rest

Cool Down

Swim Activity	Distance	Reps	Time	Rest

Difficulty: 🏊 🏊 🏊   Rating: ⭐ ⭐ ⭐ ⭐ ⭐

TRAINING LOG

Date: _____ Time: _____

Warm Up

Swim Activity	Distance	Reps	Time	Rest

Sets

Swim Activity	Distance	Reps	Time	Rest

Cool Down

Swim Activity	Distance	Reps	Time	Rest

Difficulty: 🏊 🏊 🏊 Rating: ⭐ ⭐ ⭐ ⭐ ⭐

TRAINING LOG

Date: _____ Time: _____

Warm Up

Swim Activity	Distance	Reps	Time	Rest

Sets

Swim Activity	Distance	Reps	Time	Rest

Cool Down

Swim Activity	Distance	Reps	Time	Rest

Difficulty: 🏊 🏊 🏊 Rating: ⭐ ⭐ ⭐ ⭐ ⭐

TRAINING LOG

Date: _____ Time: _____

Warm Up

Swim Activity	Distance	Reps	Time	Rest

Sets

Swim Activity	Distance	Reps	Time	Rest

Cool Down

Swim Activity	Distance	Reps	Time	Rest

Difficulty: 🏊 🏊 🏊 Rating: ⭐ ⭐ ⭐ ⭐ ⭐

TRAINING LOG

Date: _____ Time: _____

Warm Up

Swim Activity	Distance	Reps	Time	Rest

Sets

Swim Activity	Distance	Reps	Time	Rest

Cool Down

Swim Activity	Distance	Reps	Time	Rest

Difficulty:

Rating: ⭐ ⭐ ⭐ ⭐ ⭐

TRAINING LOG

Date: _____ Time: _____

Warm Up

Swim Activity	Distance	Reps	Time	Rest

Sets

Swim Activity	Distance	Reps	Time	Rest

Cool Down

Swim Activity	Distance	Reps	Time	Rest

Difficulty: 🏊 🏊 🏊   Rating: ⭐ ⭐ ⭐ ⭐ ⭐

TRAINING LOG

Date: _____ Time: _____

Warm Up

Swim Activity	Distance	Reps	Time	Rest

Sets

Swim Activity	Distance	Reps	Time	Rest

Cool Down

Swim Activity	Distance	Reps	Time	Rest

Difficulty: 🏊 🏊 🏊 Rating: ⭐ ⭐ ⭐ ⭐ ⭐

TRAINING LOG

Date: _____ Time: _____

Warm Up

Swim Activity	Distance	Reps	Time	Rest

Sets

Swim Activity	Distance	Reps	Time	Rest

Cool Down

Swim Activity	Distance	Reps	Time	Rest

Difficulty: 🏊 🏊 🏊   Rating: ⭐ ⭐ ⭐ ⭐ ⭐

TRAINING LOG

Date: _____ Time: _____

Warm Up

Swim Activity	Distance	Reps	Time	Rest

Sets

Swim Activity	Distance	Reps	Time	Rest

Cool Down

Swim Activity	Distance	Reps	Time	Rest

Difficulty: Rating:

TRAINING LOG

Date: _____ Time: _____

Warm Up

Swim Activity	Distance	Reps	Time	Rest

Sets

Swim Activity	Distance	Reps	Time	Rest

Cool Down

Swim Activity	Distance	Reps	Time	Rest

Difficulty: 🏊 🏊 🏊 Rating: ⭐ ⭐ ⭐ ⭐ ⭐

TRAINING LOG

Date: _____ Time: _____

Warm Up

Swim Activity	Distance	Reps	Time	Rest

Sets

Swim Activity	Distance	Reps	Time	Rest

Cool Down

Swim Activity	Distance	Reps	Time	Rest

Difficulty: 🏊 🏊 🏊   43   Rating: ⭐ ⭐ ⭐ ⭐ ⭐

TRAINING LOG

Date: _____ Time: _____

Warm Up

Swim Activity	Distance	Reps	Time	Rest

Sets

Swim Activity	Distance	Reps	Time	Rest

Cool Down

Swim Activity	Distance	Reps	Time	Rest

Difficulty: 🏊 🏊 🏊   Rating: ⭐ ⭐ ⭐ ⭐ ⭐

TRAINING LOG

Date: _____ Time: _____

Warm Up

Swim Activity	Distance	Reps	Time	Rest

Sets

Swim Activity	Distance	Reps	Time	Rest

Cool Down

Swim Activity	Distance	Reps	Time	Rest

Difficulty: Rating:

45

TRAINING LOG

Date: _____   Time: _____

Warm Up

Swim Activity	Distance	Reps	Time	Rest

Sets

Swim Activity	Distance	Reps	Time	Rest

Cool Down

Swim Activity	Distance	Reps	Time	Rest

Difficulty: 🏊 🏊 🏊   Rating: ⭐ ⭐ ⭐ ⭐ ⭐

TRAINING LOG

Date: _____ Time: _____

Warm Up

Swim Activity	Distance	Reps	Time	Rest

Sets

Swim Activity	Distance	Reps	Time	Rest

Cool Down

Swim Activity	Distance	Reps	Time	Rest

Difficulty: 🏊 🏊 🏊 Rating: ⭐ ⭐ ⭐ ⭐ ⭐

TRAINING LOG

Date: _____ Time: _____

Warm Up

Swim Activity	Distance	Reps	Time	Rest

Sets

Swim Activity	Distance	Reps	Time	Rest

Cool Down

Swim Activity	Distance	Reps	Time	Rest

Difficulty: 🏊 🏊 🏊   Rating: ⭐ ⭐ ⭐ ⭐ ⭐

TRAINING LOG ——

Date: _____ Time: _____

Warm Up

Swim Activity	Distance	Reps	Time	Rest

Sets

Swim Activity	Distance	Reps	Time	Rest

Cool Down

Swim Activity	Distance	Reps	Time	Rest

Difficulty: 🏊 🏊 🏊   Rating: ⭐ ⭐ ⭐ ⭐ ⭐

TRAINING LOG

Date: _____ Time: _____

Warm Up

Swim Activity	Distance	Reps	Time	Rest

Sets

Swim Activity	Distance	Reps	Time	Rest

Cool Down

Swim Activity	Distance	Reps	Time	Rest

Difficulty: 🏊 🏊 🏊 Rating: ⭐ ⭐ ⭐ ⭐ ⭐

TRAINING LOG

Date: _____ Time: _____

Warm Up

Swim Activity	Distance	Reps	Time	Rest

Sets

Swim Activity	Distance	Reps	Time	Rest

Cool Down

Swim Activity	Distance	Reps	Time	Rest

Difficulty: 🏊 🏊 🏊   51   Rating: ⭐ ⭐ ⭐ ⭐ ⭐

TRAINING LOG

Date: _____ Time: _____

Warm Up

Swim Activity	Distance	Reps	Time	Rest

Sets

Swim Activity	Distance	Reps	Time	Rest

Cool Down

Swim Activity	Distance	Reps	Time	Rest

Difficulty: 🏊 🏊 🏊   Rating: ⭐ ⭐ ⭐ ⭐ ⭐

TRAINING LOG

Date: _____ Time: _____

Warm Up

Swim Activity	Distance	Reps	Time	Rest

Sets

Swim Activity	Distance	Reps	Time	Rest

Cool Down

Swim Activity	Distance	Reps	Time	Rest

Difficulty: 🏊 🏊 🏊   Rating: ⭐ ⭐ ⭐ ⭐ ⭐

TRAINING LOG

Date: _____ Time: _____

Warm Up

Swim Activity	Distance	Reps	Time	Rest

Sets

Swim Activity	Distance	Reps	Time	Rest

Cool Down

Swim Activity	Distance	Reps	Time	Rest

Difficulty: 🏊 🏊 🏊 Rating: ⭐ ⭐ ⭐ ⭐ ⭐

TRAINING LOG

Date: _____   Time: _____

Warm Up

Swim Activity	Distance	Reps	Time	Rest

Sets

Swim Activity	Distance	Reps	Time	Rest

Cool Down

Swim Activity	Distance	Reps	Time	Rest

Difficulty: 🏊 🏊 🏊   Rating: ⭐ ⭐ ⭐ ⭐ ⭐

TRAINING LOG

Date: _____ Time: _____

Warm Up

Swim Activity	Distance	Reps	Time	Rest

Sets

Swim Activity	Distance	Reps	Time	Rest

Cool Down

Swim Activity	Distance	Reps	Time	Rest

Difficulty: 🏊 🏊 🏊

Rating: ⭐ ⭐ ⭐ ⭐ ⭐

TRAINING LOG

Date: _____ Time: _____

Warm Up

Swim Activity	Distance	Reps	Time	Rest

Sets

Swim Activity	Distance	Reps	Time	Rest

Cool Down

Swim Activity	Distance	Reps	Time	Rest

Difficulty: 🏊 🏊 🏊   57   Rating: ⭐ ⭐ ⭐ ⭐ ⭐

TRAINING LOG ─

Date: _____ Time: _____

Warm Up

Swim Activity	Distance	Reps	Time	Rest

Sets

Swim Activity	Distance	Reps	Time	Rest

Cool Down

Swim Activity	Distance	Reps	Time	Rest

Difficulty: 🏊 🏊 🏊   Rating: ⭐ ⭐ ⭐ ⭐ ⭐

TRAINING LOG

Date: _____ Time: _____

Warm Up

Swim Activity	Distance	Reps	Time	Rest

Sets

Swim Activity	Distance	Reps	Time	Rest

Cool Down

Swim Activity	Distance	Reps	Time	Rest

Difficulty: 🏊 🏊 🏊   Rating: ⭐ ⭐ ⭐ ⭐ ⭐

TRAINING LOG

Date: _____ Time: _____

Warm Up

Swim Activity	Distance	Reps	Time	Rest

Sets

Swim Activity	Distance	Reps	Time	Rest

Cool Down

Swim Activity	Distance	Reps	Time	Rest

Difficulty: 🏊 🏊 🏊 Rating: ⭐ ⭐ ⭐ ⭐ ⭐

TRAINING LOG

Date: _____ Time: _____

Warm Up

Swim Activity	Distance	Reps	Time	Rest

Sets

Swim Activity	Distance	Reps	Time	Rest

Cool Down

Swim Activity	Distance	Reps	Time	Rest

Difficulty: 🏊 🏊 🏊 Rating: ⭐ ⭐ ⭐ ⭐ ⭐

TRAINING LOG

Date: _____ Time: _____

Warm Up

Swim Activity	Distance	Reps	Time	Rest

Sets

Swim Activity	Distance	Reps	Time	Rest

Cool Down

Swim Activity	Distance	Reps	Time	Rest

Difficulty: 🏊 🏊 🏊   Rating: ⭐ ⭐ ⭐ ⭐ ⭐

TRAINING LOG

Date: _____ Time: _____

Warm Up

Swim Activity	Distance	Reps	Time	Rest

Sets

Swim Activity	Distance	Reps	Time	Rest

Cool Down

Swim Activity	Distance	Reps	Time	Rest

Difficulty: 🏊 🏊 🏊   Rating: ⭐ ⭐ ⭐ ⭐ ⭐

TRAINING LOG

Date: _____ Time: _____

Warm Up

Swim Activity	Distance	Reps	Time	Rest

Sets

Swim Activity	Distance	Reps	Time	Rest

Cool Down

Swim Activity	Distance	Reps	Time	Rest

Difficulty: 🏊 🏊 🏊 Rating: ⭐ ⭐ ⭐ ⭐ ⭐

TRAINING LOG

Date: _____ Time: _____

Warm Up

Swim Activity	Distance	Reps	Time	Rest

Sets

Swim Activity	Distance	Reps	Time	Rest

Cool Down

Swim Activity	Distance	Reps	Time	Rest

Difficulty: 🏊 🏊 🏊 Rating: ⭐ ⭐ ⭐ ⭐ ⭐

TRAINING LOG

Date: _____ Time: _____

Warm Up

Swim Activity	Distance	Reps	Time	Rest

Sets

Swim Activity	Distance	Reps	Time	Rest

Cool Down

Swim Activity	Distance	Reps	Time	Rest

Difficulty: 🏊 🏊 🏊　Rating: ⭐ ⭐ ⭐ ⭐ ⭐

TRAINING LOG

Date: _____ Time: _____

Warm Up

Swim Activity	Distance	Reps	Time	Rest

Sets

Swim Activity	Distance	Reps	Time	Rest

Cool Down

Swim Activity	Distance	Reps	Time	Rest

Difficulty: 🏊 🏊 🏊   Rating: ⭐ ⭐ ⭐ ⭐ ⭐

TRAINING LOG

Date: _____ Time: _____

Warm Up

Swim Activity	Distance	Reps	Time	Rest

Sets

Swim Activity	Distance	Reps	Time	Rest

Cool Down

Swim Activity	Distance	Reps	Time	Rest

Difficulty: 🏊 🏊 🏊 Rating: ⭐ ⭐ ⭐ ⭐ ⭐

TRAINING LOG

Date: _____ Time: _____

Warm Up

Swim Activity	Distance	Reps	Time	Rest

Sets

Swim Activity	Distance	Reps	Time	Rest

Cool Down

Swim Activity	Distance	Reps	Time	Rest

Difficulty: 🏊 🏊 🏊 Rating: ⭐ ⭐ ⭐ ⭐ ⭐

TRAINING LOG ——

Date: _____ Time: _____

Warm Up

Swim Activity	Distance	Reps	Time	Rest

Sets

Swim Activity	Distance	Reps	Time	Rest

Cool Down

Swim Activity	Distance	Reps	Time	Rest

Difficulty: 🏊 🏊 🏊 Rating: ⭐ ⭐ ⭐ ⭐ ⭐

TRAINING LOG

Date: _____ Time: _____

Warm Up

Swim Activity	Distance	Reps	Time	Rest

Sets

Swim Activity	Distance	Reps	Time	Rest

Cool Down

Swim Activity	Distance	Reps	Time	Rest

Difficulty: 🏊 🏊 🏊   Rating: ⭐ ⭐ ⭐ ⭐ ⭐

TRAINING LOG

Date: _____ Time: _____

Warm Up

Swim Activity	Distance	Reps	Time	Rest

Sets

Swim Activity	Distance	Reps	Time	Rest

Cool Down

Swim Activity	Distance	Reps	Time	Rest

Difficulty: 🏊 🏊 🏊

Rating: ⭐ ⭐ ⭐ ⭐ ⭐

TRAINING LOG

Date: _____ Time: _____

Warm Up

Swim Activity	Distance	Reps	Time	Rest

Sets

Swim Activity	Distance	Reps	Time	Rest

Cool Down

Swim Activity	Distance	Reps	Time	Rest

Difficulty: 🏊 🏊 🏊   Rating: ⭐ ⭐ ⭐ ⭐ ⭐

TRAINING LOG

Date: _____ Time: _____

Warm Up

Swim Activity	Distance	Reps	Time	Rest

Sets

Swim Activity	Distance	Reps	Time	Rest

Cool Down

Swim Activity	Distance	Reps	Time	Rest

Difficulty: 🏊 🏊 🏊   Rating: ⭐ ⭐ ⭐ ⭐ ⭐

TRAINING LOG ─────

Date: _____ Time: _____

Warm Up

Swim Activity	Distance	Reps	Time	Rest

Sets

Swim Activity	Distance	Reps	Time	Rest

Cool Down

Swim Activity	Distance	Reps	Time	Rest

Difficulty: 🏊 🏊 🏊   Rating: ⭐ ⭐ ⭐ ⭐ ⭐

TRAINING LOG

Date: _____ Time: _____

Warm Up

Swim Activity	Distance	Reps	Time	Rest

Sets

Swim Activity	Distance	Reps	Time	Rest

Cool Down

Swim Activity	Distance	Reps	Time	Rest

Difficulty: 🏊 🏊 🏊   Rating: ⭐ ⭐ ⭐ ⭐ ⭐

TRAINING LOG

Date: _____ Time: _____

Warm Up				
Swim Activity	Distance	Reps	Time	Rest

Sets				
Swim Activity	Distance	Reps	Time	Rest

Cool Down				
Swim Activity	Distance	Reps	Time	Rest

Difficulty: 🏊 🏊 🏊   Rating: ⭐ ⭐ ⭐ ⭐ ⭐

TRAINING LOG

Date: _____ Time: _____

Warm Up

Swim Activity	Distance	Reps	Time	Rest

Sets

Swim Activity	Distance	Reps	Time	Rest

Cool Down

Swim Activity	Distance	Reps	Time	Rest

Difficulty: 🏊 🏊 🏊 Rating: ⭐ ⭐ ⭐ ⭐ ⭐

TRAINING LOG

Date: _____ Time: _____

Warm Up

Swim Activity	Distance	Reps	Time	Rest

Sets

Swim Activity	Distance	Reps	Time	Rest

Cool Down

Swim Activity	Distance	Reps	Time	Rest

Difficulty: 🏊 🏊 🏊   Rating: ⭐ ⭐ ⭐ ⭐ ⭐

TRAINING LOG

Date: _____ Time: _____

Warm Up

Swim Activity	Distance	Reps	Time	Rest

Sets

Swim Activity	Distance	Reps	Time	Rest

Cool Down

Swim Activity	Distance	Reps	Time	Rest

Difficulty: 🏊 🏊 🏊   Rating: ⭐ ⭐ ⭐ ⭐ ⭐

TRAINING LOG

Date: _____ Time: _____

Warm Up

Swim Activity	Distance	Reps	Time	Rest

Sets

Swim Activity	Distance	Reps	Time	Rest

Cool Down

Swim Activity	Distance	Reps	Time	Rest

Difficulty: 🏊 🏊 🏊   Rating: ⭐ ⭐ ⭐ ⭐ ⭐

TRAINING LOG ──

Date: _____ Time: _____

Warm Up

Swim Activity	Distance	Reps	Time	Rest

Sets

Swim Activity	Distance	Reps	Time	Rest

Cool Down

Swim Activity	Distance	Reps	Time	Rest

Difficulty: 🏊 🏊 🏊 Rating: ⭐ ⭐ ⭐ ⭐ ⭐

TRAINING LOG

Date: _____ Time: _____

Warm Up

Swim Activity	Distance	Reps	Time	Rest

Sets

Swim Activity	Distance	Reps	Time	Rest

Cool Down

Swim Activity	Distance	Reps	Time	Rest

Difficulty: 🏊 🏊 🏊   Rating: ⭐ ⭐ ⭐ ⭐ ⭐

TRAINING LOG

Date: _____   Time: _____

Warm Up

Swim Activity	Distance	Reps	Time	Rest

Sets

Swim Activity	Distance	Reps	Time	Rest

Cool Down

Swim Activity	Distance	Reps	Time	Rest

Difficulty: 🏊 🏊 🏊   Rating: ⭐ ⭐ ⭐ ⭐ ⭐

TRAINING LOG

Date: _____ Time: _____

Warm Up

Swim Activity	Distance	Reps	Time	Rest

Sets

Swim Activity	Distance	Reps	Time	Rest

Cool Down

Swim Activity	Distance	Reps	Time	Rest

Difficulty: 🏊 🏊 🏊   Rating: ⭐ ⭐ ⭐ ⭐ ⭐

TRAINING LOG

Date: _____ Time: _____

Warm Up

Swim Activity	Distance	Reps	Time	Rest

Sets

Swim Activity	Distance	Reps	Time	Rest

Cool Down

Swim Activity	Distance	Reps	Time	Rest

Difficulty: 🏊 🏊 🏊   Rating: ⭐ ⭐ ⭐ ⭐ ⭐

TRAINING LOG

Date: _____ Time: _____

Warm Up

Swim Activity	Distance	Reps	Time	Rest

Sets

Swim Activity	Distance	Reps	Time	Rest

Cool Down

Swim Activity	Distance	Reps	Time	Rest

Difficulty: 🏊 🏊 🏊 Rating: ⭐ ⭐ ⭐ ⭐ ⭐

TRAINING LOG

Date: _____ Time: _____

Warm Up

Swim Activity	Distance	Reps	Time	Rest

Sets

Swim Activity	Distance	Reps	Time	Rest

Cool Down

Swim Activity	Distance	Reps	Time	Rest

Difficulty: 🏊 🏊 🏊   Rating: ⭐ ⭐ ⭐ ⭐ ⭐

TRAINING LOG

Date: _____ Time: _____

Warm Up

Swim Activity	Distance	Reps	Time	Rest

Sets

Swim Activity	Distance	Reps	Time	Rest

Cool Down

Swim Activity	Distance	Reps	Time	Rest

Difficulty: 🏊 🏊 🏊 Rating: ⭐ ⭐ ⭐ ⭐ ⭐

TRAINING LOG —

Date: _____ Time: _____

Warm Up

Swim Activity	Distance	Reps	Time	Rest

Sets

Swim Activity	Distance	Reps	Time	Rest

Cool Down

Swim Activity	Distance	Reps	Time	Rest

Difficulty: 🏊 🏊 🏊 Rating: ⭐ ⭐ ⭐ ⭐ ⭐

TRAINING LOG

Date: _____ Time: _____

Warm Up				
Swim Activity	Distance	Reps	Time	Rest

Sets				
Swim Activity	Distance	Reps	Time	Rest

Cool Down				
Swim Activity	Distance	Reps	Time	Rest

Difficulty: 🏊 🏊 🏊   Rating: ★ ★ ★ ★ ★

TRAINING LOG ——

Date: _____ Time: _____

Warm Up

Swim Activity	Distance	Reps	Time	Rest

Sets

Swim Activity	Distance	Reps	Time	Rest

Cool Down

Swim Activity	Distance	Reps	Time	Rest

Difficulty: 🏊 🏊 🏊 Rating: ⭐ ⭐ ⭐ ⭐ ⭐

TRAINING LOG

Date: _____ Time: _____

Warm Up

Swim Activity	Distance	Reps	Time	Rest

Sets

Swim Activity	Distance	Reps	Time	Rest

Cool Down

Swim Activity	Distance	Reps	Time	Rest

Difficulty: 🏊 🏊 🏊   Rating: ★ ★ ★ ★ ★

TRAINING LOG

Date: _____ Time: _____

Warm Up

Swim Activity	Distance	Reps	Time	Rest

Sets

Swim Activity	Distance	Reps	Time	Rest

Cool Down

Swim Activity	Distance	Reps	Time	Rest

Difficulty: 🏊 🏊 🏊   94   Rating: ⭐ ⭐ ⭐ ⭐ ⭐

TRAINING LOG

Date: _____ Time: _____

Warm Up

Swim Activity	Distance	Reps	Time	Rest

Sets

Swim Activity	Distance	Reps	Time	Rest

Cool Down

Swim Activity	Distance	Reps	Time	Rest

Difficulty: 🏊 🏊 🏊   95   Rating: ⭐ ⭐ ⭐ ⭐ ⭐

TRAINING LOG

Date: _____ Time: _____

Warm Up

Swim Activity	Distance	Reps	Time	Rest

Sets

Swim Activity	Distance	Reps	Time	Rest

Cool Down

Swim Activity	Distance	Reps	Time	Rest

Difficulty: 🏊 🏊 🏊   Rating: ⭐ ⭐ ⭐ ⭐ ⭐

— TRAINING LOG —

Date: _____ Time: _____

Warm Up

Swim Activity	Distance	Reps	Time	Rest

Sets

Swim Activity	Distance	Reps	Time	Rest

Cool Down

Swim Activity	Distance	Reps	Time	Rest

Difficulty: 🏊 🏊 🏊   Rating: ★ ★ ★ ★ ★

TRAINING LOG

Date: Time:

Warm Up

Swim Activity	Distance	Reps	Time	Rest

Sets

Swim Activity	Distance	Reps	Time	Rest

Cool Down

Swim Activity	Distance	Reps	Time	Rest

Difficulty: 🏊 🏊 🏊   Rating: ⭐ ⭐ ⭐ ⭐ ⭐

TRAINING LOG

Date: _____ Time: _____

Warm Up

Swim Activity	Distance	Reps	Time	Rest

Sets

Swim Activity	Distance	Reps	Time	Rest

Cool Down

Swim Activity	Distance	Reps	Time	Rest

Difficulty: 🏊 🏊 🏊 Rating: ⭐ ⭐ ⭐ ⭐ ⭐

TRAINING LOG

Date: _____ Time: _____

Warm Up

Swim Activity	Distance	Reps	Time	Rest

Sets

Swim Activity	Distance	Reps	Time	Rest

Cool Down

Swim Activity	Distance	Reps	Time	Rest

Difficulty: 🏊 🏊 🏊 Rating: ⭐ ⭐ ⭐ ⭐ ⭐

——PERSONAL RECORDS——

Date	Swim Style	Distance	Time

—PERSONAL RECORDS—

Date	Swim Style	Distance	Time

PERSONAL RECORDS

Date	Swim Style	Distance	Time

—PERSONAL RECORDS—

Date	Swim Style	Distance	Time

— PERSONAL RECORDS —

Date	Swim Style	Distance	Time

— PERSONAL RECORDS —

Date	Swim Style	Distance	Time

━ PERSONAL RECORDS ━

Date	Swim Style	Distance	Time

—PERSONAL RECORDS—

Date	Swim Style	Distance	Time

— PERSONAL RECORDS —

Date	Swim Style	Distance	Time

— PERSONAL RECORDS —

Date	Swim Style	Distance	Time

— PERSONAL RECORDS —

Date	Swim Style	Distance	Time

—PERSONAL RECORDS—

Date	Swim Style	Distance	Time

—PERSONAL RECORDS—

Date	Swim Style	Distance	Time

—PERSONAL RECORDS—

Date	Swim Style	Distance	Time

—PERSONAL RECORDS—

Date	Swim Style	Distance	Time

—PERSONAL RECORDS—

Date	Swim Style	Distance	Time

NOTES

NOTES

NOTES

NOTES

NOTES

NOTES

NOTES

NOTES

NOTES

NOTES

NOTES

NOTES

NOTES

NOTES

NOTES

NOTES

NOTES

NOTES

NOTES

NOTES

Made in the USA
Middletown, DE
18 December 2020